Pets at the Vet

By Alyse Sweeney

Children's Press®
A Division of Scholastic Inc.
New York Toronto London Auckland Sydney
Mexico City New Delhi Hong Kong
Danbury, Connecticut

These content vocabulary word builders are for grades 1–2.
Subject Consultant: Mary M. Christopher, DVM, PhD, Professor, University of California–Davis School of
Veterinary Medicine, Davis, California

Reading Consultant: Cecilia Minden-Cupp, PhD, Former Director of the Language and Literacy Program,
Harvard Graduate School of Education, Cambridge, Massachusetts

Photographs © 2007: age fotostock/Frank Siteman: 9; Alamy Images/Thorsten Eckert: 2, 4 bottom left, 10;
Animals Animals/Peter Weimann: 20 right; AP/Wide World Photos: 21 bottom (Jessie Cohen/National Zoo),
21 top (Douglas C. Pizac), 20 left (James Poulson/Daily Sitka Sentinel); Corbis Images: back cover, 11 (Jim
Craigmyle), 23 bottom left (Frank Lukasseck/zefa), 1, 4 top, 19 (LWA-JDC), 23 bottom right (Joe McDonald),
23 top left (Robert Pickett), 4 bottom right, 8, 13, 17 (Royalty-Free), 23 top right (Stuart Westmorland); Getty
Images/Kaz Mori/The Image Bank: 5 bottom left, 15; Masterfile/Jerzyworks: cover; Photo Researchers, NY:
5 bottom right, 16 (John & Maria Kaprielian), 5 top right, 12 (Astrid & Hanns-Frieder Michler); photolibrary.
com/Mendil/Bsip: 5 top left, 7.

Book Design: Simonsays Design!
Book Production: The Design Lab

Library of Congress Cataloging-in-Publication Data

Sweeney, Alyse.
  Pets at the vet / by Alyse Sweeney.
    p. cm. — (Scholastic news nonfiction readers)
  Includes bibliographical references and index.
  ISBN-10: 0-531-16811-5
  ISBN-13: 978-0-531-16811-0
  1. Veterinary medicine—Vocational guidance—Juvenile literature.
  2. Veterinarians—Juvenile literature. I. Title. II. Series.
  SF756.28S94 2007
  636.089023—dc22   2006015657

1 2 3 4 5 6 7 8 9 10 R 16 15 14 13 12 11 10 09 08 07

CONTENTS

WORD HUNT

Look for these words as you read. They will be in **bold**.

cast
(kast)

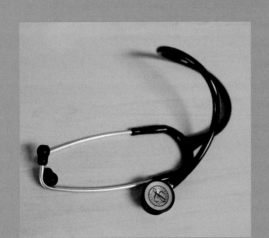

stethoscope
(**steth**-e-scope)

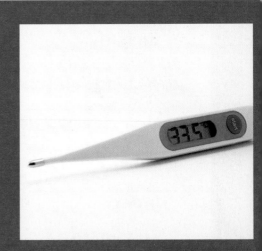

thermometer
(ther-**mom**-et-er)

This vet checks to see if the cat's eyes are healthy.

This dog is here for a checkup, too! It sits on a scale to be weighed.

Then the veterinarian will take the dog's temperature with a **thermometer**.

thermometer

The veterinarian will be happy. This dog weighs just the right amount.

Has a doctor ever listened to your heart and lungs with a **stethoscope**?

A veterinarian uses this tool to listen to an animal's heart and lungs, too.

stethoscope

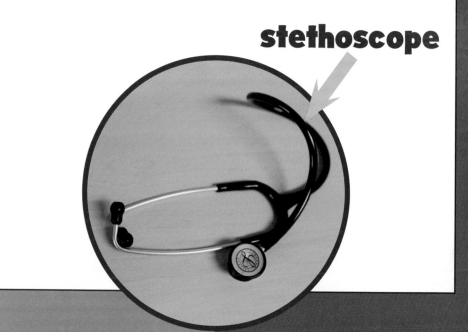

This cat has a strong heartbeat!

Pets get **medicine** just like you do.

When your pet is sick, the veterinarian finds just the right medicine.

The medicine helps your pet get well.

medicine

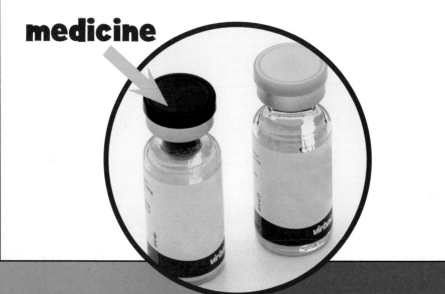

This veterinarian will give the birds some of the medicine on the shelf.

Did you know that veterinarians are animal dentists, too?

That's right. An animal can get a cavity just like you.

That's why veterinarians clean their patients' teeth at each yearly checkup.

This veterinarian looks at the dog's teeth and gums.

Oh no! A dog was rushed into the veterinarian's office.

The dog hurt its leg.

The veterinarian uses a machine to take an **X-ray** of the dog's leg.

The X-ray shows a broken bone!

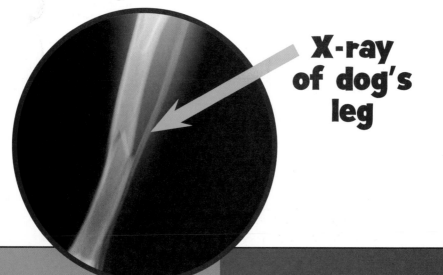

X-ray of dog's leg

Vets look at the dog's X-ray and talk about what they see.

The veterinarian puts a **cast** on the dog's leg to help the bone heal.

It's been another busy day at the veterinarian's office!

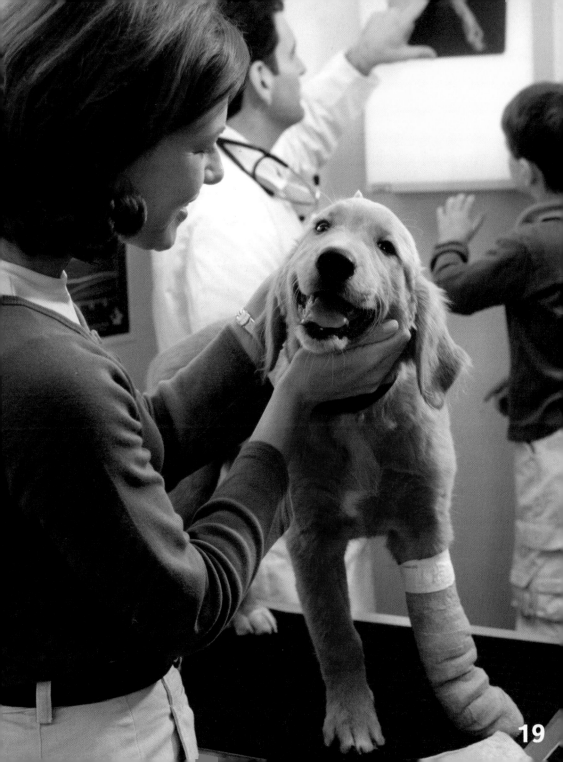

ALL KINDS OF VETERINARIANS

aquarium veterinarian

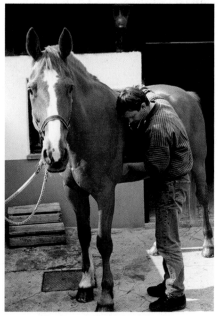

large animal veterinarian

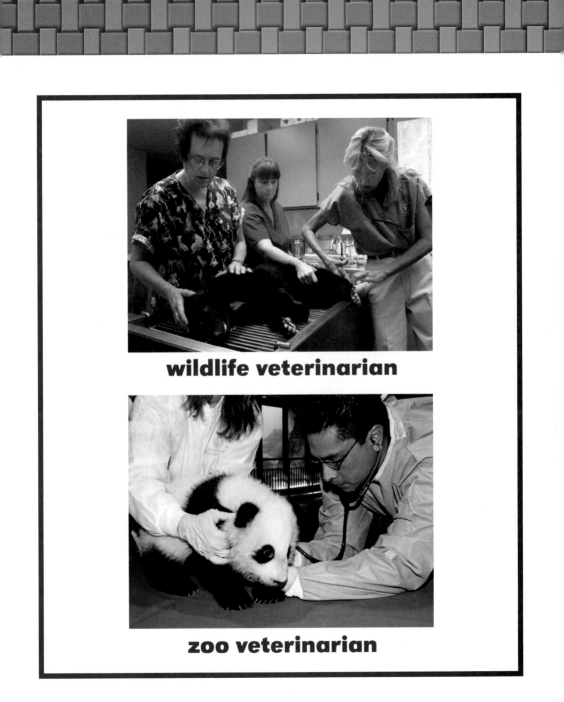

wildlife veterinarian

zoo veterinarian

YOUR NEW WORDS

cast (**kast**) a hard covering that helps a broken bone heal

checkup (**chek**-up) a visit to a doctor or veterinarian to make sure a person or animal is healthy

medicine (**med**-eh-sin) something given to people or animals to make them better when they are sick

stethoscope (**steth**-e-scope) a tool used for listening to the heart and lungs

thermometer (ther-**mom**-et-er) a tool used for measuring temperature

veterinarian (vet-er-e-**nare**-ee-un) a doctor who helps animals stay healthy

X-ray (**eks**-ray) a picture of the inside of the body

OTHER PETS AT THE VET

hamster

parrot

rabbit

turtle

23

INDEX

FIND OUT MORE
Book:
Englart, Mindi Rose, and Melanie Stengel (illustrator). *Veterinarian*. San Diego: Blackbirch Press, 2003.

Website:
Coast and Country Veterinarians Kidz Zone
http://www.thevets.com.au/kidz_zone.htm

MEET THE AUTHOR:
Alyse Sweeney is a freelance writer who has published more than twenty books and poems for children. Prior to becoming a freelance writer, she was a teacher, reading specialist, and Scholastic editor. Alyse lives in Las Vegas, Nevada, with her husband and two children.